Read for a Better World™

DOCTORS
A First Look

PERCY LEED

GRL Consultant, Diane Craig, Certified Literacy Specialist

Lerner Publications ◆ Minneapolis

Educator Toolbox

Reading books is a great way for kids to express what they're interested in. Before reading this title, ask the reader these questions:

> What do you think this book is about? Look at the cover for clues.

> What do you already know about doctors?

> What do you want to learn about doctors?

Let's Read Together

Encourage the reader to use the pictures to understand the text.

Point out when the reader successfully sounds out a word.

Praise the reader for recognizing sight words such as *to* and *for*.

TABLE OF CONTENTS

Doctors 4

Doctors

Doctors help people
feel better.
They help people who
are sick or hurt.

Doctors work
with nurses.
They work together
to help people.

There are many types
of doctors.
Some help new moms.

Others work with bones.

Doctors may wear
face masks.
Masks help to
keep people safe.

How do masks keep people safe?

11

Many doctors wear white coats. This shows people they are doctors.

Doctors use tools.
This tool lets
doctors hear our
hearts.

stethoscope

What other tools do doctors use?

Doctors talk to people.
They ask questions.

They think about what each person needs.

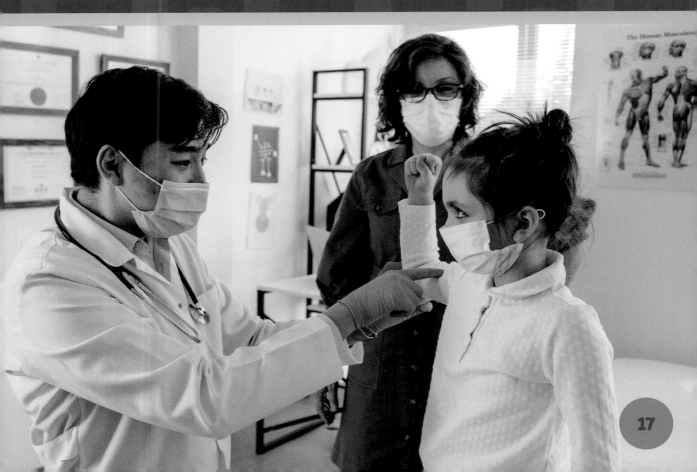

Doctors go to school for many years.

Why must doctors go to school?

Doctors work hard to care for people!

You Connect!

What is something you like about doctors?

How has a doctor helped you?

Would you like to be a doctor when you grow up?

Social and Emotional Snapshot

Student voice is crucial to building reader confidence. Ask the reader:

What is your favorite part of this book?

What is something you learned from this book?

Did this book remind you of any community helpers you've met?

Photo Glossary

coat

mask

nurse

stethoscope

Learn More

Bender, Douglas. *Doctor*. New York: Crabtree Publishing, 2022.

Boothroyd, Jennifer. *All about Doctors*. Minneapolis: Lerner Publications, 2021.

Waxman, Laura Hamilton. *Doctor Tools*. Minneapolis: Lerner Publications, 2020.

Index

Photo Acknowledgments

The images in this book are used with the permission of: © FatCamera/iStockphoto, pp. 4–5, 9, 14–15, 16, 18–19; © SDI Productions/iStockphoto, pp. 6–7, 12–13, 20, 23 (bottom left, top left); © Prostock-Studio/iStockphoto, p. 8; © Geber86/iStockphoto, pp. 10–11, 23 (top right); © catinsyrup/Shutterstock Images, pp. 14, 23 (bottom right); © Phynart Studio/iStockphoto, p. 17.

Cover Photograph: © SDI Productions/iStockphoto

Design Elements: © Mighty Media, Inc.

Lerner Publications Company
An imprint of Lerner Publishing Group, Inc.
241 First Avenue North
Minneapolis, MN 55401 USA

For reading levels and more information, look up this title at www.lernerbooks.com.

Main body text set in Mikado a Medium.
Typeface provided by Hannes von Doehren.

Library of Congress Cataloging-in-Publication Data

Names: Leed, Percy, 1968–author. | Craig, Diane, consultant.
Title: Doctors: a first look / Percy Leed ; GRL Consultant, Diane Craig, Certified Literacy Specialist.
Description: Minneapolis : Lerner Publications, [2025] | Includes bibliographical references and index. | Audience: Ages 5–8 | Audience: Grades K–1 | Summary: "Doctors help us when we are sick or hurt. Full-color photographs and leveled text help young readers learn more about these very important community helpers"–Provided by publisher.
Identifiers: LCCN 2023031821 (print) | LCCN 2023031822 (ebook) | ISBN 9798765626405 (lib. bdg.) | ISBN 9798765629529 (pbk) | ISBN 9798765636763 (epub)
Subjects: LCSH: Physicians—Juvenile literature.
Classification: LCC R690 .L435 2025 (print) | LCC R690 (ebook) | DDC 610.92—dc23/eng/20231207

LC record available at https://lccn.loc.gov/2023031821
LC ebook record available at https://lccn.loc.gov/2023031822

Manufactured in the United States of America
1 – CG – 7/15/24